Copyright © 2021 Zayne Francis

All rights reserved

The characters and events portrayed in this book are fictitious. Any similarity to real persons, living or dead, is coincidental and not intended by the author.

No part of this book may be reproduced, or stored in a retrieval system, or transmitted in any form or by any means, electronic, mechanical, photocopying, recording, or otherwise, without express written permission of the publisher.

ISBN: 9798486286223

Cover design by: Art Painter
Library of Congress Control Number: 2018675309
Printed in the United States of America

CONTENTS

Copyright
Preface
Chapter 1   3
Chapter 2   11
Chapter 3   16
Chapter 4   21
Chapter 5   24
Chapter 6   30
Chapter 7   38
Chapter 8   44

PREFACE

The one question I continually receive from the men I mentor: "Is there any strategy I can implement today to overcome self doubt, fears, discouragement, and most often, feeling stuck?"

This is a major problem in our modern world for men. The question then becomes. Why is it we get stuck, what are the obstructions holding men back from our highest selves, and how can we go about preventing them? That's a multifaceted question that this book is designed to answer for you. Providing all subsets needed for success, boundaries, order, and men in our modern world. Guiding you not only outwardly, but inwardly. As a man.

Through virtue, devotion, archetypal alignment, science, fitness, and practical methodology, all applied correctly, this information and strategy integrated eventually invokes vocation. Breaking through any barriers blocking abundance, redirecting toward a worthy ideal.

Welcome to Subsets of Success, Money, and Mastery.

Zayne Francis

CHAPTER 1

The Subsets of Success in our Modern World

Feeling stuck, lost, is simply a by-product of having no outward output in order to sustain momentum. Often, this is due to the lack of a practical practice that allows you to create it. Momentum breeds joy within ourselves, and about what we're doing in our lives. This applies to exercise, your vocation, and anything you do. A quick remedy to this stagnant state is having the proper exercise and eating routine to uphold this flow, creating more energy; which will ultimately reflect into all other aspects of yourself, life, business, and relationships. We all know this, as this is fundamental. The focal point of all action in our world. Every action is driven through the sentiment at which it proceeds. You only attract, generate, and create what you are, your life is a direct extension you. Who are you being? This habitual ability practiced, will catalyze the ability to uphold and sustain commitments and decisions within ourselves; as exercise and training the mind and body, reflects everything we practice. We need a direct plan for implementing action, and sustaining this. This is exactly why I always visit training and eating with my clients first and foremost. Let's dig a bit deeper into this topic for a minute.

As the men I mentor question me, I find the most common issue is these men are being too hard on themselves. Due to many underlying issues. Our indulgences, our habits, our actions. All play in to exactly who it is you're being, or not being. What I see happen most often through the thousands of sessions I've practiced with men, the most common problem still presents itself. The common denominator of the issue as I observe it, is having trouble living up to your own value system, resulting in a degree of self hatred. The quickest remedy to this, would be the firm training routine. Something that's a practical practice, builds momentum, catalyzes more commitments, and highly transformative on every level. Training is just as metaphysical, as it is physical.

If you already uphold a value system

within, that's already half the battle! Most lack this sense of self, and base to work from to begin with. Many can't even find themselves in a firm enough place to begin. Perhaps that's you. It doesnt have to be. That alone is empowering. You're already beyond this. Here's where you begin.

As an prior martial artist and competitive powerlifter myself, I can tell you, daily lifting and movement is still essential to our growth, strength, and development as men, for not only ourselves, but the extension of ourselves. The ability to protect and provide for our families, inside, emotionality, presence, and outwardly in our worlds activites and experiences. To experience our lives in their wholness, to the greatest intended degree, we must uphold these commitments. Why? They keep us grounded, focused, and joyful. Think of them as our personal debt we owe to the creator for having this incredible experience. The least you can do for yourself, and those around you, is to maintain your physical ablities. Reflecting ability to recieve and reciprocate emotion, connection, and expansion in every area of life. Here's why training is reflecting just as much metaphysical exercise, as it is physical.

Training our minds and bodies in the gym, helps us overcome stress and tension physically, mentally, and spiritually. If we can break barriers within ourselves physically through training in the gym, this reflects breaking barriers metaphysically within our character and our lives. Of course, this will reflect in our relationships, social situations, and families. You choose to do the hard things, you get an easy life. You're already one step ahead of the game.

You should ENJOY training, as you progressively get better, you acquire a taste for challenging activity.

Why? Because you start seeing progress, you break through physical and mental tensions and barriers, and you start becoming the all around, strongest and integrated version of yourself. Cultivating ourselves physically is a spiritual practice at the essence.

Character Structure

Character structure is very important to understand in the context of exercise, and how it's correlated with how we show up in the world. Our character structures are essentially the health of our character, through its physical manifestation. Within our bodies. Unconsciously, our characters form the habits sustained by our bodies.

The state of our minds, is only a reflection of the state of our bodies. If we're constantly sitting, hunched over, have backpack back, or due to any reasons whatsoever, these positions cement into our character.

If you're hunched over, you're going to be shut down and closed off. This leads to a constricted and closed heart center, and eventually, these neurotic holding patterns are what manifest further disease within us down the line.

Through the openness, working through these holding patterns and blocks, and reaching the fullest expressions of ourselves within our bodies, we can move throughout this reality, fully and freely, grounded within our masculine presence and essence. I'm going to give you many exercises to be able to work towards opening any blocks you may find within your body, that are literally restricting your fullest expression, and your true character.

Here's how we begin to work with ourselves further reintegrating and reshaping our own character structures.

CHAPTER 2

A Firm Frame Is a Firm Mind, Is a Firm Life.

Our bodies are one giant interconnected system, constantly communicating, transmitting, and receiving data, you're often not consciously aware of. Without having and upholding a firm frame to move throughout this world, we lose many of our most vital elements that make us men. First being our character structures, the traits that have become apart of us, and reflect how we show up in the world, due to many factors. First, the food we eat, as well as the habits sustained within this area of our lives. Ever heard the saying 'If you can control your diet, you can control your life'? Well, it's true.

You want to eat healthy and optimally, in the most primal way possible as in documented history/religion? Try fasting.

Recent studies are not only proving fasting to work like true magic for the mind and body, but it clears us of the main consumption pattern that we sustain throughout the day. This clears subconscious baggage, the mind, and the body. Our bodies have a natural flush system, and fasting properly activates this, sending our bodies into an entire full body-brain cleanse.

Fasting develops the mind, cleanses the spirit, in this way, we gain the ultimate clarity. It helps us to be open to receive revelations about ourselves, our lives, allowing us to view ourselves and indulgences from multiple different angles. This allows our life path to open to us, through being truly revealed and be properly led. If you don't understand what I mean yet, you will piece it together through the concepts I deliver throughout the upcoming chapters. Here's how we allow our lives to unfold, as we get out of our own way.

Let's dive deep into reaching this state of alignment, in order to truly be led through right action.

Most people eat as an emotional crutch, another way of stuffing and suppressing feelings. Fasting helps us clear them all, face them properly, and gain momentum in the direction of clearing all addictions.

These pent up emotions are often what are keeping you stuck feeling lazy, unmotivated, unable to focus, overthinking, and lacking clarity. It's unconscious baggage. You become hyper aware of your emotions, through abstaining from feeding that one large consumption pattern. This allows us to address them, work through them, and clear them properly.

We'll go into how to actually get yourself going training and fasting with tools I'll provide later. But first, we must understand how we're to begin being led in the right directions within our lives. Through alignment, your true self and path are revealed to you through revelation. The direction you must take, is usually right in front of you. In your case, it's this book.

When we reach this state of alignment, we can begin to discern important things. Like the difference between right action vs activity, and what is to be discarded vs the work that is our true life's calling.

We cannot understand and take right action, without the integration of The Law of Pure Potentiality. We cannot understand The Law of Pure Potentiality and its power, fully, without interconnecting Archetypal Masculinity with our understanding. These next few chapters will help you receive these concepts at their full magnitude.

CHAPTER 3

The Law of Pure Potentiality

There is a law in quantum physics called The Law of Pure Potentiality. Moving unresourceful obstructions from our lives allows this law to open up to us. We've created the space to receive. The understanding of drawing down pure potential, what this actually looks like from an Archetypal and fundamental level, is essential for success beyond anything you can conceptualize with your conscious mind. Because, it's just that. Pure potentiality. You can't guess it. Beyond your wildest imaginations.

The law itself states: Anything beyond our wildest imaginations has the ability to manifest at any time. That is the beauty of life here on earth, pure potential. To unlock this pure potentiality of our reality, we must clear out all activity bred from the wrong sentiment of action. Learning to be still. Just as important as action, as we learned earlier, is pure stillness. "Every man's problems, proceed from his inability to sit. Alone. In a room, by himself, with his thoughts." Just as important as what we're doing in order to sustain momentum, is the polarization of this. Who we're being. Taking the time to simply, be. We're not human doings, for a reason. Being is of our essence.

What this means is, we must STOP things that are merely surface level activities we may think are propelling us forward, but are merely blinding us further with their cycles. This is why fasting aids so much during this process, it's a non doing process. Clearing out unresourceful activity, in order to reveal what is.

When we attach to an idea, a thought, or an outcome, and take action out of the sentiment of those projections and fears instead of sitting, and being open; immediately we lose this potentiality of our reality and collapse back into a reality.

Right action is of your SOUL, not outside projections. RIGHT ACTION is the plan you want to rely on. The plan is of you, and will be revealed when we align in these ways.

The path is counterintuitive. We're led to believe we must grit, grunt, and grind our way to what we want. This isn't the case. Exactly what we want and deeply desire, is a knowing deep within that has the ability to be reflected outwardly. In developing these character traits, commitment systems, and value structures, we can come home to ourselves. Our actions will be led out of the sentiment of our soul, not outside projections you've absorbed and applied onto yourself. For example, things you've seen others doing. Maybe something your parents said you should do, or an activity you practice you believe is propelling you forward, that may be mere mind masturbation. The idea is that through clearing all of the unresourceful activities bred from false fears, hopes, and dreams of others, we can lead our actions out of alignment, and right action. What

God has truly designated us to do here.

Through the patterning of the father, we can atone and align with our highest selves, leading our highest paths. Most of our activities nowdays are pointless. Leading us no further in depth of understanding, facilitating further growth. Instead, much of our world treats activity as gluttony. Here's how we properly discern right, true, real action, vs mind masturbation, and activity.

CHAPTER 4

IDENTIFYING Right Action

There are many things to do, many courses to take, many books to read, that the most sane thing we can possibly do, is focus down on one particular thing until it's done. Going tunnel vision. Clear out all other unresourceful actions when working toward a worthy ideal.

The actions you may be inclined to take

within your life, may not be right actions. We all sometimes struggle with the distinguishment and discernment between right action, and activity. Some things we find ourselves doing, are merely activities. Bred from ideas, stories, and thoughts you've held and projected onto yourself through others. An idea you've held an attachment towards is an example. Whatever it may be, your reality forms to pertain to the desired outcomes of those realities. This collapses us back into a reality, closing off the law of pure potentiality as we learned earlier. A thought is a reality. We must not get caught here, as our reality is truly infinite when we're open to receiving its blessings.

This book is what you need to take action on. It's right in front of you. This will fill your cup up, in order for it to pour into the gift your life holds for you to offer.

Focus down on this study. In a generation of so much activity, so many things, so many distractions, we lose focus.

The most sane thing to do is focus on ONE big thing, and let your path follow as it unfolds for you.

CHAPTER 5

Archetypal Alignment

You will never be filled with a sense of momentus pleasure in your life, be balanced, or self actualized, without having the inner Warrior quality truly devoted to serving the inner King by subjecting himself to his higher calling. Here's what I mean.

Robert Moore delivered a reformation of the idea of the four male qualities, four modes of being, one in which men are always operating. The archetype goes, the King, the Warrior, the Magician, and the Lover. These labels are to describe the quadrated psyche, and help us understand the four modes of being we hold. The King quality is simply Being. The Warrior quality is Doing, the Magician quality is Thinking, and the Lover quality is Feeling. We're always doing one of these things, or operating within one of these modes. It is rare now with our society of vast distractions and so many things to do, that we can just be. This is because we become heavily attached to the three modes of being that keep us from doing just that. When we stop taking senseless action, as we've learned, we can hold all of this kinetic energy on reserve through practicing stillness. Holding reserves, in order for the force to be applied in the time of right action.

When right action ensues, you know. Its of you, and moves through you. It will be revealed to you once you work to align in these ways, this is 90% of the battle.

In our generation due to our free love and freely sexually expressive society, as well as a myriad of other byproducts of this industrialized civilization; we are most wounded in our Lover. We become overly attached to our feelings, and in turn we develop unhealthy attachments to the things that bring us a sense of pleasure. Our inner lovers are extremely over inflated. We're way too addicted to our feelings. This is how we become so heavily attached to the things that make us feel good, and bring a pleasurable sensation. Our pleasures are most often our addictions. The number one for most men, happens to be pornography.

Nobody gets out of our industrialized civilization without a wounded Lover. Every single one of us at some point have become addicted or attached to something unresourceful, even unconsciously within your life.

Self awareness is being aware of these addictions, how much of our energy is being put towards these things, directions, and mitigating the exposure as much as possible. At least to the point what you're doing is not a crutch, it's a tool.

What do I mean by your path 'Unfolding'?

The right action for you to take will be spoken into you. Vocation = Voice. When you align in the ways I'm teaching you today, your next action to take will soon be revealed to you. It's a byproduct of this action you're taking now, the return investment of this book you invested in. You are on the right path. You do not need a scripted plan in order to get from where you are to where you want to be. This is actually HOLDING YOU BACK from getting there, as we learned through the law of pure potentiality. This programs your actions and decisions to pertain to that desired outcome, when your true self knows what you truly desire, and exactly how to guide you into getting there. That's how you made it here.

This is why integrating stillness is so important. When right action ensues, we can recognize it. Stillness isn't the least bit empty. It is pregnant with pure potential. Reigning the potentiality stillness withholds, you're able to apply all necessary force in the right directions when right action ensues.

CHAPTER 6

Importance of Stillness

Stillness as we've learned helps us tap into our utmost potential, by truly being able to hear ourselves. This is fundamental to being led in the right directions within life, and hold a connection with our true selves. We're far too heavily clouded through many meaningless stimulations, sensations, pleasures, that people forget they have an internal navigation system built within them.

We must take the time to clear out, and listen.

Be a dam on the verge of collapsing before you take action, with all of your kinetic energy and force ready to be applied in the time of right action. When right action ensues, you know.

Nonjob (Your own business) Goals

Men must have a plan. Find something you can tolerate. Or even better, something you enjoy doing, and make money doing that. We're taught we must always feel a sense of passion about what we're doing. Your vocation and passion don't always need to be the same, nor are they linked. I believe this pulls us in many unresourceful directions.

Take this idea for example. If we tire out our passions by constantly having to practice them, they won't be passions anymore. We can also override great opportunities if we're simply not feeling that passionate feeling. That's just a feeling. We can't always sustain it, so its not practical to rely on. Commitment, discipline, delayed gratification, and virtues are what we must rely on instead. So maybe, its best to find practical work, that pays for now, and your true path will unfold before your eyes as you develop further. Showing up, doing the work to your fullest, acting as if it is your own. This is how we truly connect with our purpose as men. Find the joy and momentum within the work.

We must lay out a few practical nonjob goals in order for you to apply this knowledge and start climbing it yourself.

1. Mindset Training.

You must not place anything above you. The moment you do this, you cannot have it. "Your potential is likley 16x what you're currently making." - Stefan Aarnio.

2. Develop A Journal

With your most important tasks, prioritize. I cannot stress this enough. Break down your daily goals into small tasks, and watch them blossom. The smallest tasks you know you need to do every single day, do them first.

3. Lay Out The Foundations.

Set high preformance 90 day, and long term goals. Long term goals are great to have, but we must always focus on whats in front of us, and the path will be revealed as we work on what we know needs done. Design these goals to be in Health, Wealth, and Happiness. Credit to Stefan here as well, RIP. We must clearly define what it is we want, after being revealed. What is it God has spoken into you through this process, that now you can draw down and apply? If not anything yet, all you need to do, is take the time to be still. Allow it to reveal itself.

Breaking Unresourceful Connections - To GROW YOUR WINGS.

There are some connections you're not meant to sustain with certain people, because those connections are simply unresourceful. Nothing but another anchor holding you back from the highest version of yourself, and path for your life. The like minded men I resonate with, resonate with me.

You're the manifestation of the five people you surround yourself with the most, choose to be around the right group of people. COHESIVE COMMUNITY! Men truly need other men in order to be highly successful, it's our nature. We lift eachother up alongside one another. I am you, you are me. Nothing is more resourceful than making true connections, especially with other strong men.

Dealing With Childhood Trauma - Parental Forgiveness

Forgiving your mother and father for what they may have not done or what they may have done, is the first and healthiest step to take in regaining a fully functioning, healthy, relationship between you.

There may be unresolved tensions left unsaid, and things that need to be brought up. This is all in holding a grounded, human connection with your parents as an adult. Dealing with the things that are still bothering you, and moving forward with the relationship by bringing value. Chances are if they are willing to engage with you in these things i've listed, they're desiring a totally healthy relationship between the two of you.

The quality of the relationship you had with your mother and father, and the unresolved feelings and traumas associated with them, could ultimately reflect within your personal relationships subconsciously. You want to be aware of these patterns, notice them, and not allow them to influence your actions within your relationships. You want to remain stoic, a rock for your partner to lean on. This is a properly balanced polarization dynamic within a relationship.

You definitely do not want unresolved parental traumas presenting and projecting themselves onto your relationships within your adult life. Get it out of the way with them!

If the situation in the home you live with your family is simply too toxic, you must break away from this; as its fundamentally holding you back from your highest self. Every man must leave home at some point, Better sooner rather than later.

Jump off that cliff, get out of the mud, and reconnect with yourself. If you can't do this yet, that's alright, establish boundaries. This will reflect within the respect your family has for you. PROTECT YOUR PEACE AT ALL COSTS!

CHAPTER 7

Integration In Order to Receive - You ARE The Plan

As you integrate and work through these lessons and extract the knowledge to be received, you'll begin to notice you show up differently. People will begin to treat you differently, as your perception of yourself begins to shift. Along with this, will come the opportunity for new relationships with quality people. These lessons will become a part of you.

Foundations for Future Generations - Leave Your Legacy

You want to reserve yourself, find the right woman, and plan for fatherhood. This is the most natural thing for a man to do, and will leave the legacy of his name forever. Men are naturally protectors and providers, as women are naturally nurturers, homemakers and caretakers. This is our natural order, and is exactly what our world is trying to destroy. Why? Because its POWERFUL. Men and women are better TOGETHER. To be a father, is to be a KING. An adequate protector, procreator, and provider of a safe space for the people around him to flourish.

Your purpose, and the purpose of life itself isn't something outside of us to be sought after or searched for. The meaning is simply BEING.

Try just being present in this moment. Fully immersed in the arms and chair, just sitting. Just sit, and see what comes to mind. This also helps us ground ourselves within the present moment further. To experience this whole reality for what it has to offer us when we open up to it. Don't search for the meaning. BE the meaning!

The meaning again, is within simply being. Present. In this moment of consciousness. Same goes with your purpose. When being, still, unmoved, it will be spoken into you, because it's OF you. Nothing outside of you.

We're led and conditioned to believe that the meaning is outside of us. This is a generational lie, and a trap. This keeps us wrongfully searching, running away from what's truly here for us in this present moment.

MASCULINE VIRTUE - The Hero's Journey

There are masculine virtues, and feminine virtues. There are masculine traits, and feminine traits. When it pertains to intersexual dynamics, being grounded within your center and founded around masculine virtue means you can properly show up in the world as a full embodiment of a masculine figure. You reflect your actions out in the world, and into the relationships you attract into your life. Also, your ability to properly sustain them.

In our world, there is a pervasive force at hand attacking masculinity. We must work to uphold this in our fallen world. MASCULINE VIRTUE is the key to this.

Some examples of Masculine Virtue are discipline, commitment, devotion, courage, and decisiveness. These determine the energy you hold, how you present yourself in the world, and the actions that are reflected back out within it. We must uphold masculine virtue in order to abstain from things like porn, and any other indulgences designed to destroy us. This keeps us showing up as the men we're truly meant to be. Our fullest selves.

There comes a time in every man's life where he must face what's referred to as 'The Hero's Journey'. This is the time in which we must slay our dragons. The dragons of fear, shame, guilt, doubt, whatever it may be. We've gotta slay that dragon. It's usually behind doing the things we're afraid to do, that we destroy these barriers within us.

The quickest remedy to self doubt, is doing the thing you're afraid to do. If you do the thing, you will have the power.

This new sense of life that will be given to you as a result, will ultimately shift you into the newest version of yourself and your life. After you've slayed that dragon!

CHAPTER 8

Successful People Make Their Decisions Right

I never imagined I would write books such as I have, but I was led. It was of the right action, of my path and a higher devotion than myself. It was my moral obligation to fulfill this duty of my higher calling, and it brought forth the most miraculous things in my life. You're about to experience the same through this book. Learning to be still, take right action, and hold higher commitments, values, virtues, devotions. You'll be ultimately led exactly to where you need to be, when you need to be there.

You shouldn't be worried about making the right decision, you should be worried about making no decision. The difference between successful people and others, are not right decisions. Successful people make all kinds of bad decisions, the difference between successful people and others, is that successful people make their decisions right. COMMIT! TAKE ACTION! If you have the inspiration to do something, that's your calling! DO IT, and see what happens! It's never about what you get, it's about who you're becoming along the way. Who you're being, or who you're not being.

Discipline, commitment, and strong habits, are what gets things done, and generates overall success. They propel us forward in many small ways. Adding a layer brick by brick to our ability to uphold, maintain, and keep those habits. This is in order to sustain and create success over a prolonged period of time. This is also going to reflect in your character, as these are very masculine actions and traits. Choose ONE THING to commit to doing EVERYDAY whether you feel like it, or not, and start developing this habitual ability within you. You'll then gain confidence in yourself, and your ability to create more habits.

SELF DOUBT = CRUSH Self Doubt to Maintain Habits, Momentum, and Progress.

The men I've worked with have delivered a recurring theme of a similar question. Self doubt. How do we remedy this? Like I said earlier, the remedy to self doubt is doing that thing. The thing you are doubting. From that, will come gems.

Worries about not succeeding? No need to worry! Worrying will only slow down the process of clearing out in order to hold the utmost light. We attract the frequency we hold, and our experiences are produced by the habits that uphold our frequency.

Our bodies have a built in system that regulates our experiences and traumas. It stores those feelings associated with them, within our subconscious minds. In this case, the mind is the body, so these pent up issues reflect many things.

Maintain Focus, Prioritizing Time, Family, Work, Workouts, etc.

Maintaining focus is all about prioritizing it. Often we lose focus doing the things that matter, because we spend too much time doing the things that don't. ALWAYS prioritize. Prioritize your work, your workouts, your time with family, your time with your partner. Whatever it may be, PRIORITIZE!! I cannot stress this enough!

We are only human, not machines, and we have limits. We must prioritize to get things done optimally, and on time. Especially to maintain stress levels, because we often easily stress ourselves out over expecting too heavy of a workload. To uphold our work, we must choose what's most important, tackle it, and then focus on the rest in your spare time.

Assessments to KEEP You Focused to Succeed

- DO NOT DO LIST ~ There is a huge value in intolerance, as we're openly being conditioned to be tolerant to very real issues. This causes a shutdown of our personal virtuous barriers and walls. In reality, this leaves us unable to grow a garden. We must establish what we will NOT do. Write down at least 10 things you vow never to do again. This in and of itself is momentum, without really having to do anything, or take any action, other than abstaining. You'll feel clearer, and able to see your path with less noise and distractions. This will give you the ability to take true decisive action on your soul goals, and keep that momentum going.

- Read a book! Reading is a fundamental element to ourselves, our inspiration, and expanding our awareness. Outside, and within. Books themselves provide their own incredible revelations, and ideas. When applied in your life and the gold nuggets extracted properly, you can experience similar things through a book, that you would a course. This is just the bare beginning for you!

- Get your first training course/routine for your needs and desires, and take ACTION!

- After this fast, write down your SOUL GOALS, the things that are truly being spoken into you through this stillness, and revelations that are pointing you in the right directions.

Thank you for reading, and taking action toward your greatest self.

Read other work by Zayne:

Sacred Sexuality: How Pornography Has Disrupted our Sacred Relationships, Lives, and Families. Reinstalling Our Lost Core Virtues of Sacred Sexuality.

Sacred Masculinity: Guide to Mature Masculine Revival in Love, Meaning, and Leading.

RETHINK Adderall & ADHD: Ulterior

ZAYNE FRANCIS

Psychological Sources of Biological Behavioral Expressions.